Hymns 16
Original Sacred SATB Music
Volume 16

Music Copyright 2019 by Kevin G. Pace

Texts copyright 2019 by Mark Fotheringham,
Angie Killian, Kathryn Hales, & Mary Ann Snowball
as noted in this book.

PaceMusicServices.com

Hymns 16
Original Sacred SATB Music
Volume 16

A Mother There

Music: Kevin G. Pace & Angie Killian
Text: Angie Killian

Peacefully =66
1. My heart yearns Her con - nec - tion, A chance to know Her
2. I see Her in the col - ors That dance on paint - ed
3. I smell in pink car - na - tions Her soft and sweet bou -
4. I see Her in the ag - ing, In chil - dren as they
face, Her gen - tle - ness and hol - i - ness, The warmth of Her em -
wings, In bloom - ing hues that fill my view When win - ter yields to
quet And feel her breeze give life to trees On te - pid, sun - ny
grow, In hush - ing cries and lul - la - bies, And an - gels down be -
brace. I search Her in my pin - ing And find Her ev - 'ry
spring. I hear Her in the song - birds' Me - lod - ic gifts to
days. I taste Her in the crisp - ness Of sum - mer's first picked
low. I won - der if she smi - les When strang - ers show they
where, For all the world re - minds me: I have a Moth - er there.
air,
pear.
care,

Let All Creation Praise His Coming

Music: Kevin G. Pace
Text: Mary Ann Snowball

Joyfully ♩=72
1. Let all cre-a-tion praise His com-ing, Send-ing tri-umph through the sky!
2. So, let the earth burst forth re-ver-ing; Let the wa-ters cheer with praise.
3. Let all the stars and morn-ing sun-beams Sing to-geth-er, all as one.
4. Let his cre-a-tions call for one-ness To de-clare his name with love,

When Je-sus Christ steps from the Fa-ther All the heav-ens will sup-ply
Let all the moun-tains shout for glad-ness All be-cause our Lord was raised.
Let all the woods and trees and mead-ows Voice their joy be-cause He comes.
And to pro-claim the voice of Je-sus When He vis-its from a-bove.

Grand al-le-lu-ias to all lis-t'ning And those long a-wait-ed sounds
Let all the val-leys hear re-joic-ing And the seas and dry lands bring
Then let the an-i-mals speak joint-ly, And the sun and moon share light;
Let all cre-a-tion praise His com-ing For his light will be our sun;

Will an-nounce the Sec-ond Com-ing When His glo-ry will a-bound.
Grand-est strains to all for-ma-tion Be-cause He is Christ, our King.
Let the whole world join in wor-ship Be-cause He is in our sight.
Let us shout with hymns of sing-ing Be-cause Christ, our Sav-ior comes!

Remember

Music: Kevin G. Pace
Text: Mark R. Fotheringham

Worshipfully ♩=92

1. Re - mem - ber, re - mem - ber, there are things you once knew From be -
2. Re - mem - ber, re - mem - ber, you are wrapped in God's love. You are
3. Re - mem - ber, re - mem - ber, that God of - fered His Son, Who would
4. Re - mem - ber, re - mem - ber, there's a place where you go To e -
fore you were born to a world new to you. And
known here be - low, you are loved from a - bove. Though
teach you to love. He a - toned for each one. You
ter - nal - ly live and con - tin - ual - ly grow. Un -
al - though now hid - den a - way from clear view, Your
long you have tra - veled to come from a - far, Your
fol - low His foot - steps as each truth you learn, Re -
til you re - turn there to reap what you sow, Re -
spir - it re - mem - bers when you find some - thing true.
Heav - en - ly Fath - er knows and loves who you are.
pen - tant and faith - ful, so with joy you'll re - turn.
mem - ber, re - mem - ber, ev - 'ry truth you may know.

The Shepherd and The Lamb

Music: Kevin G. Pace
Text: Mary Ann Snowball

Joyfully ♩.=42

1. Be - fore the first, small breath of life On that first Christ - mas day, The
called the fish - er - men at sea; He taught up - on the Mount. He
soon He was the Lamb Him - self, Who died to cleanse our stains. His
on - ly, and e - ter - nal work, He gave for us in love! If

ti - ny, ba - by Je - sus knew He would pre - pare the way. From
was the car - ing Shep - herd and His lost sheep did He count. At
blood He spilt so will - ing - ly To take a - way our pains. Why
we will heed the Shep - herd's call We'll be with Him a - bove. He

ear - ly morn - ing's gen - tle sun Till dusk's more shad - owed cast, He
times He found one gone a - stray, Or lost in dark and cold. He'd
would this man, this per - fect Son, Who stands first at the gate, De -
was the sac - ri - fi - cial Lamb, And Shep - herd all in one, For

1, 2, 3.

grew and walked the dust - y paths, And blessed all whom He passed. 2. He
lis - ten for a small, faint cry, Then gath - er close to hold. 3. But
sire to pay that price for us, A sac - ri - fice so great? 4. His
from his first breath to his last, He

17
4.
was the prom - ised Son. He was the Shep - herd
20
and the Lamb; He is our sav - ing One.

Please Forgive Me

Music: Kevin G. Pace
Text: Mary Ann Snowball

Pleadingly ♩=66

1. Please for-give me, God a - bove; Pu - ri - fy my heart. Please let me be
2. Please re-lease me from his grasp; I can't bear the pain. I im - plore Thee
3. Heav'n - ly Fa - ther, can Thou sense My re - li - ance on My dear Sav ior,
4. Send thy love through Him a - lone; Take my ache a - way. Please, dear Fa - ther,

safe in Thee, And to gain a part Of thy spe - cial
night and day For e - rase of stain. Ease my trou - bled
Je sus Christ? To him I be - long. Let me trust his
give me peace On this ver - y day. Let my love to

ten - der care Prom - ised from thy Son. Please, oh please, for -
mind, I beg; Sanc - ti - fy my soul. Please, know of my
prom - ised grace; Let my heart be calm. Please dear Fa - ther,
Thee be shown Through re - pen - tance true. Please for - give my

give my faults 'Til the tempt - er's done.
hon - est plea: Please let me be whole.
up a - bove, Send his heal - ing balm.
ev - 'ry sin Then I can be new.

My Savior Lives!

Music: Kevin G. Pace
Text: Mary Ann Snowball

Reverently ♩=72

1. He lives! He lives! My Sav - ior lives! I know He lives for me. He
2. He lives! My Sav - ior res - cued me. He groaned in ag - o - ny. His
3. He lives! He lives! My Sav - ior lives! His zeal can nev - er fail. He
4. My Sav - ior lives to save my soul. He lives so I shall be His

lives to save be - cause He died In cruel Geth - se - ma - ne. He
blood He spilled for all my sins; He bled to set me free. He
of - fered all his will to God Through pains from pierc - ing nails He
heir through all e - ter - ni - ty; He paid the price for me. My

lives to car - ry my sore pain And o - ver come my grief. When
cried with throbs when no one saw; His flesh was torn a - part. My
lives for me; My Sav - ior lives! I know be - cause I feel Pure
tears are wet; My hands are clasped, And I am on my knees To

I am seized by Sa - tan's grasp, He lives to give re - lief.
Sav - ior lives so I can feel His love with - in my heart.
tes - ti - mo - ny burn - ing bright; I know to Him I'm sealed.
wor - ship with my head bowed low. I know He lives for me!

How Do We Thank Our Precious Lord?

Music: Kevin G. Pace
Text: Mary Ann Snowball

Reverently ♩=84

1. How do we thank our pre - cious Lord Be - cause He gave us all?
2. Up - on the sac - ri - fi - cial throne A sweet re - mem - ber - ing
3. He prom - is - es to give us life Through all e - ter - ni - ty.
4. How do we thank our pre - cious Lord In all we do and say?

How do we sac - ri - fice for his Great ran - som from the Fall?
Brings to our minds the Sav - ior's gift Be - cause He is our King.
We'll of - fer him our bro - ken hearts And wrongs so we'll be free.
We give Him all He's giv - en us; Our ver - y wills dis - play

What cost must we give will - ing - ly To be his right - ful heir? And
His name we take up - on us and His cov - e - nants we keep So
His bod - y broke and blood was spilled; He of - fered sac - ri - fice. His
Sub - mis - sive hearts and read - y minds. We lend Him all our souls Be -

how much love can we sup - ply As He ar - rests our cares?
we can have the Ho - ly Ghost; God's bless - ings we will reap.
love be - came the cat - a - lyst; His bod - y was the price.
cause He gave his best to us; His gift lets us be whole!

9
Repentance
Music: Kevin G. Pace
Text: Mary Ann Snowball
Pleadingly ♩=84

1. Where is my soul? Where is my heart? Where is my pure in - tent?
2. Pav - il - ions sought for rest e - merge, Be - cause his love ap - pears.
3. This cost de - mands my giv - ing all - Sub - mis - sion, will - ing - ly.
4. Christ prom - ised his a - ton - ing blood; His pores would pure - ly bleed.
5. I will re - ly on Je - sus Christ; He is the on - ly Way.

Where is my pay - ment back to him For blood which Je - sus spent?
I know He has om - nis - cient sight And wants me to be near.
The gift that on - ly He be - stows Be - comes my ach - ing plea.
I know He loves me to the end; He is my Guide, my Lead.
He spent his life be - cause of love; I'm in his heart to stay.

Where is my cov - ered hid - ing place No mor - tal eye can see,
But when my soul is lost and lone, Will I re - fuse to stall?
To be for - giv - en through his pow'r Is what my heart de - sires.
He suf - fered all; His bod - y tore Be - cause of my dear soul.
I will re - mem - ber how He died; He gave all He could give

When I con - fuse the nat - u'ral man With truths so taught to me?
Can I look up, re - mem - ber - ing, The ran - son for the Fall?
Oh, change me to a crea - ture new By lend - ing sa - cred fire.
My sins can be for - giv - en when I pay the price in whole.
So my re - pent - ance will be sure; He died so I can live!

©Copyright 2019 by Kevin G. Pace & Mary Ann Snowball
PaceMusicServices.com

Be Still, And Know That I Am God

Music: Kevin G. Pace
Text: Mary Ann Snowball

Peacefully ♩=60
1. Be still, and know that I am God. Be still, and you will hear Sweet
2. Be still, and know that I am God. Be still, and you will see The
3. Be still, and know that I am God. Be still, and you will feel A
4. Be still, and know that I am God. Be still, so you'll be-lieve The
words of com-fort in your mind. Be still; I will be near. I'll
maj - es - ty of hea-ven nigh. Be still; I know your plea. I
rest - ful balm and cleans-ing cure. Be still, for I will heal. I'll
pur - est love I've ev - er giv'n. Be still; to you I'll cleave. Be
give you res - pite through the storms. My car - ing voice will speak. True
watch when pain and hurt are real. I watch you as you cry. My
wrap you in my arms of love. All flesh is in my hands. Please
still and let your heart know rest. Be still; I am the way. Be
thoughts I'll give to you a - lone For an - swers which you seek.
prom - ise is to for - ti - fy; I'll stay right by your side.
trust in my most ten - der care; I'll aid you as you stand.
still and feel my char - i - ty So peace with you will stay.

Our Savior Also Died

11
Our Savior Also Died
Music: Kevin G. Pace
Text: Mary Ann Snowball
Joyfully ♪=96

1. When oth - ers pass a - way from us Where is the strength for us to trust? Where
2. When oth - ers pass on to the grave, Our Sav - ior brings a way to save. Mor -
3. Our Sav - ior al - so died in pain So through his per - fect life we'd gain. He
4. When oth - ers pass a - way we see Through Christ, our Sav - ior, we can be Much

is the rest that will not cease? Or prom - ise of last - ing peace? Where
tal - i - ty is not the end; He gave the sure way to mend. "Come
suf - fered ev - er will - ing - ly To lend us his pow'r to see. His
clos - er to Him with each sting. Then we of - fer praise and sing: "Our

is the hope of end - less sight? When will this shad - ow change to light? How
un - to Me," His whis - per speaks, "And you will find the calm you seek. Come
ag - o - ny up - on the cross And in the Gar - den mas - tered loss. Our
Sav - ior al - so died for us; In Him we can com - plete - ly trust. He'll

will de - spair dis - cov - er calm? Where is the Lord's true heal - ing balm?
feel my pow - er yet to heal; My end - less love is meant to seal."
Sav - ior al - so died to show The bless - ing of true peace we'll know.
heal our pain; in song we'll burst Be - cause we know that He died first."

What Matchless Love

Music: Kevin G. Pace
Text: Mark R. Fotheringham

Prayerfully ♩=66

1. What match - less love is here man - i - fest.
2. Geth - se - ma - ne, a gar - den di - vine;
3. Je - sus the Christ, who hung on the cross,
4. "Thy will be done" and "Fath - er for - give."

God sent His Son, all man - kind to bless.
There Christ a - toned for your sins and mine.
He saved us all; He count - ed no cost.
These words were His, to teach how to live.

He taught of love, 'mid trou - ble and strife.
No man can know His suf - fer - ing sore.
He, hav - ing tread the wine press a - lone,
Help us re - call His beau - ti - ful choice.

He is the Way, The Truth, and the Life.
A - go - ny's press drew blood from each pore.
Vic - tor - y won, He lives on en - throned.
Help us re - call that we may re - joice.

Longing For Home

Music: Kevin G. Pace
Text: Kathryn W. Hales

Lovingly ♪=96
1. There is a place we all yearn for, No mat - ter where our paths may roam. That
2. Now let that long - ing ex - tend up - ward To our Heav - n'ly Fath - er's home, Where
spot on earth like no oth - er, That spe - cial place that we call home. It
we came from be - fore our birth, And may re - turn though far we roam. An
sym - bol - i - zes hope and com - fort, Be it hum - ble, small, or grand, The
in - ner yearn - ing fills our bos - oms, To find that peace - ful, ho - ly place, Where
cen - ter of our heart - felt long - ings; It seems the best in all the land.
par - ent - al arms will en - cir - cle In wel - com - ing and warm em - brace.

Because He Sees

Music: Kevin G. Pace
Text: Mary Ann Snowball

Tenderly ♪=96

1. When Je - sus taught the mul - ti - tudes So man - y gath - ered 'round.
2. At first He did not see me there; The crowd had joined en masse.
3. Then, nev - er to ad - just my stare Be - came my ear - nest plea.
4. To me it was a mir - a - cle That I was sin - gled out!

But I had sinned and was a - fraid To hear his ut - tered sounds.
But soon He looked right in my eyes; His care I could not pass.
As I re - turned his pre - cious gaze I felt that I was free.
I know his love is his great gift; Of this I have no doubt.

Piano/organ only

I on - ly want - ed, just one time To look up - on his form,
How could it be? He caught my glance And I could on - ly see,
My heart no long - er want - ed sin; His love was all I knew.
For - ev - er I will look to him; He lives e - ter - nal - ly.

So I hid qui - et - ly and watched One ver - y ear - ly morn.
As I looked in his ten - der eyes, Love fo - cused right at me.
His pierc - ing, but so gen - tle eyes Were all I had to view.
The love He spills to you and me Is ours be - cause He sees!

"Why Weepest Thou?"

Music: Kevin G. Pace
Text: Mary Ann Snowball
Joyfully =66

1. So ear-ly on that Sab-bath morn, Be-fore the dawn a-rose,
2. When they ar-rived, the stones were gone; The sep-ul-cher was bare.
3. And then the res-ur-rect-ed Lord Did ask Him-self this time:
4. "All hail, all hail" soon shout-ed peace A-cross the ho-ly land,

Two wo-men took their oil lamps To where the tomb was closed.
An an-gel said, "Why weep-est thou?" To Mar-y stand-ing there.
"Why weep-est thou?" Then Mar-y turned; His face was so sub-lime!
For God would wipe all tears a-way To bring the joy He planned.

They car-ried spic-es to an-noint Be-cause their Lord had died. Just
"He is not here" were dread-ed words. "But Je-sus lives a-gain!" "He
"Ra-bon-ni" was her cry a-loud; She saw her ris-en Lord! She
Christ's res-ur-rec-tion of-fers life Be-cause our Sav-ior died. We

days be-fore, in ag-o-ny, He had been cru-ci-fied.
lives! He lives! would soon be heard by all of mor-tal men.
was the first to wit-ness Him; Her love would now re-cord.
glo-ry in his per-fect gift; In Him we will a-bide.

16
You Can Change
Music: Kevin G. Pace
Text: Kathryn W. Hales
Hopefully =69
1. You can change and re-pent, Yea, turn un-to Me, E-ven though your past life, Dark and
2. You might be like James, My ver-y own broth-er, Who came to ac-cept Me as
3. You may al-ways change, Sin-cere-ly re-pent, I will lead you straight a-long On the
trou-bled may be. You may be like Saul, Per-se-cu-tor of old, Who be-
Sav-ior, no oth-er. You can be like Tim-o-thy, A Greek taught in his youth, Who
nar-row path I went. I see your po-ten-tial What some-day you may be, When Ce-
came a sure wit-ness, Known as Paul so bold.
saw with new eyes Re-vealed gos-pel truth. You can change and re-pent, Yea,
les-tial glo-ry can be yours e-ter-nal-ly.
turn un-to me, Let my grace en-fold you, Your Sav-ior I will be.
©Copyright 2019 by Kevin G. Pace & Kathryn W. Hales
PaceMusicServices.com

Jesus in Gethsemane

Music: Kevin G. Pace
Text: Mark R. Fotheringham

Solemnly ♩=72

1. Je - sus in Geth - se - ma - ne found a place to pray,
2. Pain and sor - row he en - dured, more than man could bear,
3. When at last the cup was drained, when the price was paid,

Know - ing what was soon to come, sought an - oth - er way.
Suf - fer - ing for ev - 'ry sin, ev - 'ry hurt and care.
Mer - cy now could claim it's own, ev - 'ry man to aid.

"Fath - er take this cup from me," begged a faith - ful Son.
Fac - ing ev - 'ry grief a - lone, filled his heart with dread.
Vic - to - ry for all man - kind! Bless - ed be the Lamb!

"If there be no oth - er way, then, Thy will be done.
Sweat and blood from ev - 'ry pore stained his gar - ment red.
He who suf - fered all for us is the great I Am.

Who is This Mary?

Music: Kevin G. Pace
Text: Mary Ann Snowball

Joyfully ♩=92
1. Who is this Mar - y, moth - er dear? Who is this
2. "Fear not," for God was with her now To bring forth
3. Then Mar - y pon - dered all these things And kept them
vir - gin fair? Who is this cho - sen
his own Son. For she o - beyed in
in her heart. The won - der of the
ves - sel With her at - trib - utes so rare?
ev - er - y way; This was the Ho - ly One.
prom - ised vow Of which she'd be a part
She heard the words of Gab - ri - el, The
"Be - hold the hand - maid of the Lord, ac -
Dis - tilled up - on her mind and soul. Of

an - gel from on high: "Hail, thou art
cord - ing to thy word," Was Mar - y's
wom - en she was blessed. Who is this

high - ly fa - voured." And her needs would be sup -
sure re - sponse that day; God's love would for her as -
moth - er for God's Son? From all she was the

plied.
sured.
best.
Who is this moth - er, cho - sen

first? Sweet Mar - y was most blessed.

To Be Like Joseph

Music: Kevin G. Pace
Text: Mary Ann Snowball

Gratefullly ♩=80

1. Be - fore the birth of Je - sus True Jo - seph was be - trothed To
2. With - in his heart he pon - dered His love for her so true. Oh,
3. Now, Jo - seph was the guard - ian For Mar - y's first - born Son - A
4. So, when un - planned oc - cur - rence Give chal - lenge to our days, We

Mar - y, his com - pan - ion, For they had made an oath.
could he keep the rul - ing And al - so love her too?
fore - or - dained po - si - tion To help the Ho - ly One.
may re - mem - ber Jo - seph, To keep God's sa - cred ways.

Jew - ish code and rit - u - al Re - quir - ed strict - est laws.
While he thought up - on these things An an - gel came at night
Jo - seph was se - lect - ed more Than an - y oth - er man
As we pon - der in our hearts Our pur - pos - es to share

So when Mar - y was with child, Her Jo - seph on - ly paused.
To re - lieve his trou - bled mind; He soon knew what was right.
To help rais - ing Je - sus Christ; This was the Fa - ther's plan.
We can learn, like Jo - seph did, God keeps us in his care.

On the Road to Bethlehem

Music: Kevin G. Pace
Text: Mary Ann Snowball

Ploddingly ♩=72

1. On the road to Beth - le - hem, Mar - y great with child,
2. Jew - ish cus - tom called for all Claim - ing res - i - dence
3. Mar - y's Ba - by would be born In this ver - y town.
4. On our road to Beth - le - hem, When our trek is long,

Was the lit - tle fam - i - ly, Walk - ing man - y miles.
To an - ces - tral homes re - port, So they meek - ly went.
In a cave near an - i - mals She would lay Him down.
Crowd - ed in our dai - ly life Will we, too, be - long

Out of Naz - a - reth they went, Up from Gal - i - lee.
Streets were crowd - ed but the trek, Proph - e - sied be - fore,
And be - cause the Pass - o - ver Came that ver - y week,
To the Sav - ior's fam - i - ly? Will we choose his way?

With the throngs they made their way, Plod - ding pa - tient - ly.
Wit - nessed that this "House of Bread" Was the prom - ised door.
We're re - mind - ed con - scious - ly Of the gift we seek.
On our road to Beth - le - hem He shows us the way.

A New Star Rising

Music: Kevin G. Pace
Text: Mary Ann Snowball

Joyfully ♪=80
1. A new star ris - ing, way up a - bove Shone
2. A new star ris - ing, like none be - fore, Did
3. This new star ris - ing filled heav - en - ly skies It

in the heav - ens, filled with God's love. It was a sign the
bring bright hope with bless - ings in store. For this new light dis -
lent such bright - ness, lift - ing up eyes. It led the wise - men

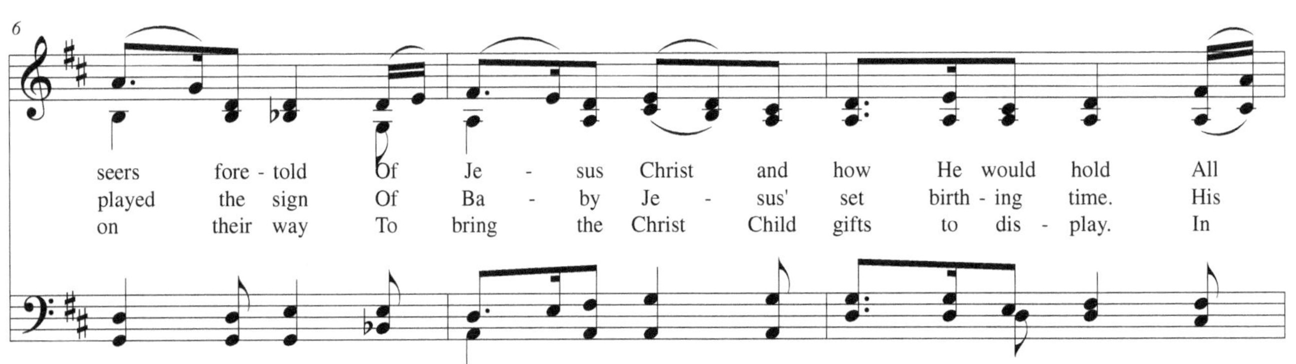

seers fore - told Of Je - sus Christ and how He would hold All
played the sign Of Ba - by Je - sus' set birth - ing time. His
on their way To bring the Christ Child gifts to dis - play. In

life in his hands, for He would be King, To gov - ern the earth by
life would be filled with tor - ment and strain, All to di - min - ish our
heav - ens a - bove the true sign was shown So Je - sus, the Christ would
rul - ing all things. It showed the Fa - ther's proph - e - sied plan Of
cries and our pain. This new star ris - ing calmed ev - 'ry heart, And
al - ways be known. Now He is called the bright, morn - ing star, Known
bring - ing res - cue to all mor - tal man.
gave each soul new peace to im - part. Now Je - sus Christ reigns
to most peo - ple, from near or from far.
from up a - bove, And is our Sav - ior filled with great love.

In Shepherd's Fields

Music: Kevin G. Pace
Text: Mary Ann Snowball

Joyfully ♩=80

1. With shep - herds sit - ting in the fields, Small lambs were gath - ered 'round. While
2. The glo - ry of the Lord dis - played A bril - liant light so new. An
3. "And this shall be a sign to you: The pre - cious Babe will stay Wrapped
4. They went with haste to find the place Where Je - sus was a - sleep. Then

keep - ing watch in dark of night Were mere noc - tur - nal sounds. Ex -
an - gel said, "Fear not; Be - hold. Good ti - dings come to you. For
all in swad - dling clothes and in a man - ger He will lay." The
mak - ing known to all a - broad, The shep - herds' love grew deep. They

pect - ing on - ly stars to glow, Soon they were sore a - fraid. To
un - to you is born this day The Sav - ior of the world. Great
heav'n - ly host praised God and said, "All glo - ry to his name. On
were the first to hear that night An - nounce - ments of his birth. 'Round

their a - maze - ment, an - gels came; Rich cho - rus - es they made.
joy to all shall come; Be still. His love will be un - furled."
earth have peace; good will t'ward men." For all He brave - ly came.
shep - herd's fields, with lambs so close, Our Sav - ior came to earth!

Turn Your Heart

Music: Kevin G. Pace
Text: Mark R. Fotheringham

Joyfully ♩=80
1. Turn your heart and seek for truth. Find the Lord while still in youth.
2. Search the scrip - tures ev - 'ry day. Feel the Spir - it point the way.
3. Live to serve your fel - low man As you fol - low heav - en's plan.
Let the Spir - it find a place to touch your heart and mind.
Rev - e - la - tion comes to those who o - pen up the heart.
Reach - ing out to lift and bless will fill your soul with light.
Bless - ings are re - served for you When you choose to live true.
When you kneel in hum - ble prayer, Know the Lord will be there
Fol - low - ing our Sa - vior Lord, Strive to live by His word.
Seek to fol - low Je - sus Christ and leave the world be - hind.
Fill - ing you with love and joy, the strength to do your part.
Em - u - late His match - less love. You'll ev - er choose the right.

I See Jesus

Music: Kevin G. Pace
Text: Kathryn W. Hales

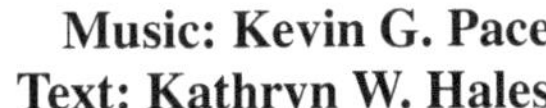

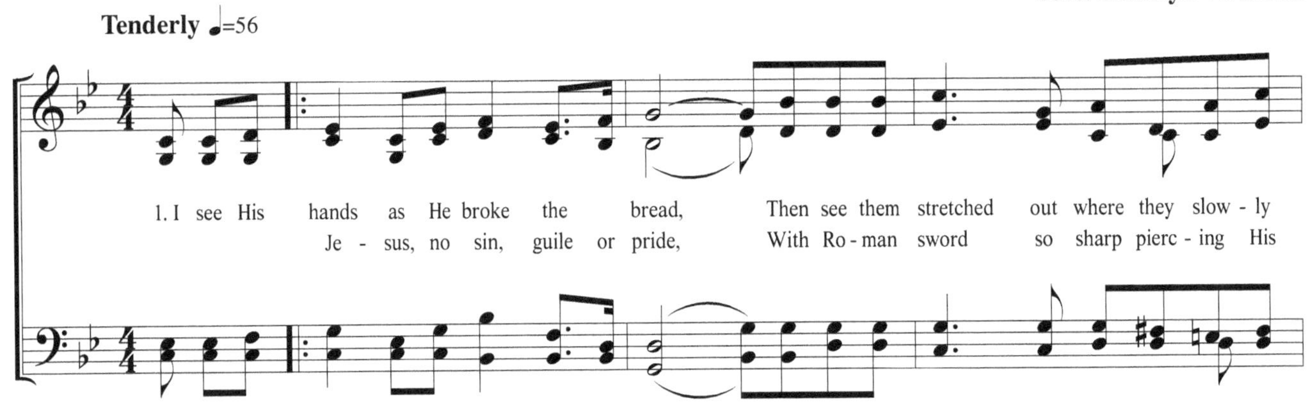
Tenderly ♩=56
1. I see His hands as He broke the bread, Then see them stretched out where they slow-ly
Je-sus, no sin, guile or pride, With Ro-man sword so sharp pierc-ing His

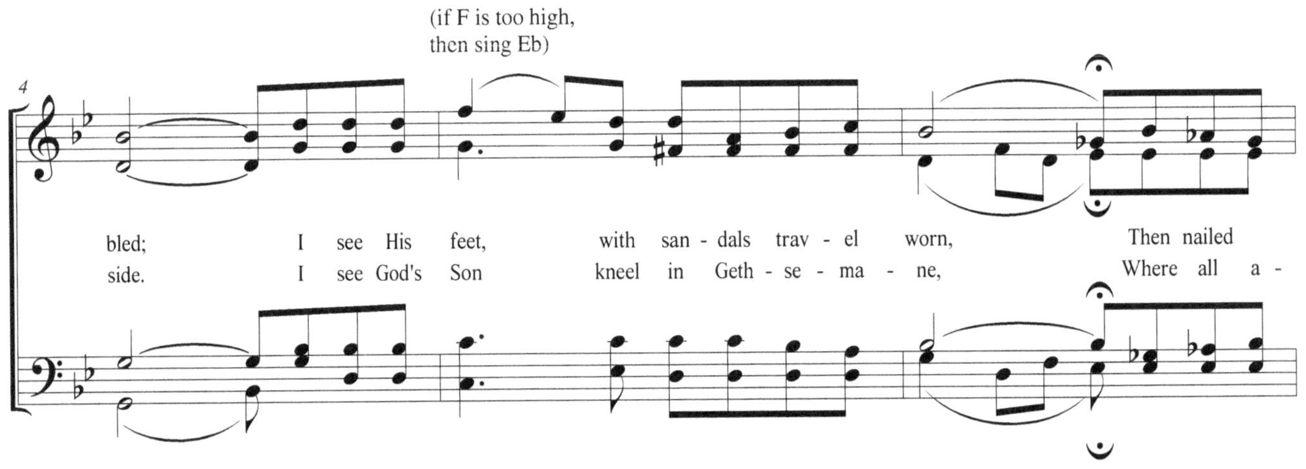
(if F is too high,
then sing Eb)
bled; I see His feet, with san-dals trav-el worn, Then nailed
side. I see God's Son kneel in Geth-se-ma-ne, Where all a-

to a cross for all who have been born. I see His hum-ble brow in fer-vant
lone He suf-fered for sin-ners like me, Shrill mock-ing scorn with meek-ness Je-sus

prayer, Then crowned with sharp thorns, much sor-row to bear. I see His
bore That He might o - pen Heav-en's gold-en door, That some-day
gen - tle face with love un - feigned. Then etched in ag - o - niz - ing grief and
I might see and know His
1.
pain. 2. I see Lord
2.
face, With wel-come arms I'll feel His warm - em - brace.
rit.

Put On the Armor of Light

(Romans 13:12, Ephesians 6:10-17)

Music: Kevin G. Pace
Text: Kathryn W. Hales

Joyfully ♩=84

1. Put on the ar - mor of Light, Be val - iant and read - y to
2. Put on the ar - mor of Light, The fu - ture will al - ways look
3. Pro - tect your ar - mor of Light; By keep - ing your goals in

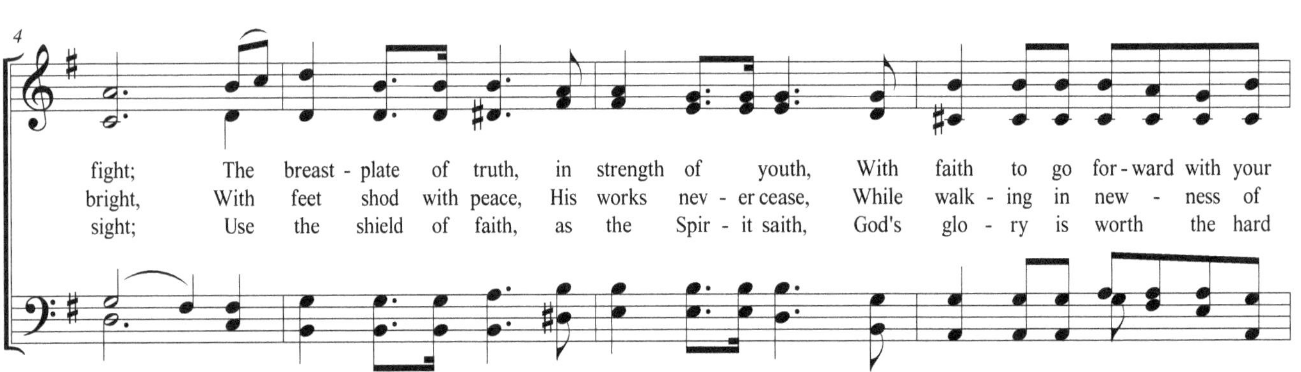

fight; The breast - plate of truth, in strength of youth, With faith to go for - ward with your
bright, With feet shod with peace, His works nev - er cease, While walk - ing in new - ness of
sight; Use the shield of faith, as the Spir - it saith, God's glo - ry is worth the hard

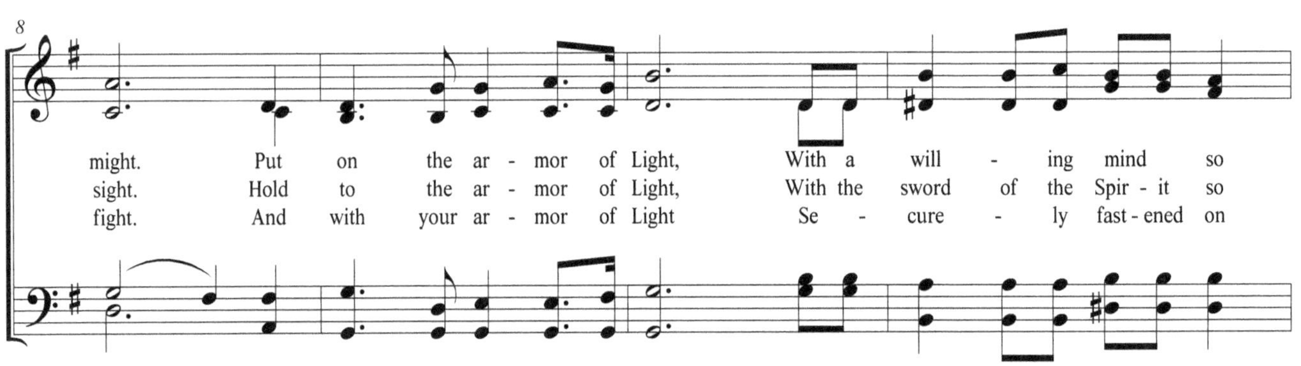

might. Put on the ar - mor of Light, With a will - ing mind so
sight. Hold to the ar - mor of Light, With the sword of the Spir - it so
fight. And with your ar - mor of Light Se - cure - ly fast - ened on

bright;   Of - fer sal - va - tion to ev - 'ry na - tion; This
tight;   Hear the small voice and make the right choice, Do
tight,   You have what's need - ed to tru - ly suc - ceed, To

hel - met brings peace and right.   Put on the ar - mor of Light; Cast
good works with sin - cere de - light.
don robes of cel - es - tial white.

off the dark - ness of night.   The Light is the Son, the

Ho - ly One, Shun e - vil by choos - ing the right.

Disciple of Christ

Music: Kevin G. Pace
Text: Mark R. Fotheringham

Gratefully ♩=72

1. Ris - ing from prayer, the spir - it set free, The
2. Pon - der His Word and hold to it fast. Plant
3. May your re - pent - ance, hon - est and true, Make
4. Sim - ply to live and hon - or His name, Will

an - swer now clear to who you must be. Dis -
deep in your heart the seeds He will cast. So
hum - ble your heart and cour - age im - bue To
bring you to God, your soul to re - claim. En -

ci - ple of Je - sus, His will to make known, You must
nour - ish your neigh - bor with fruits of the soul That the
tes - ti - fy bold - ly and go where He wills, As the
dure ev - 'ry ob - sta - cle set in you race, As His

fol - low His Way as your own.
love of the Lord you may know.
truth ev - er bright He re - veals.
coun - ten - ance shines from your face.

Biographies

Kevin G. Pace is an award-winning composer who has written over 1000 pieces of music. He specializes in choral music and piano solos and duets from beginning to advanced. He has written in many different styles including classical, modern, boogie, blues, pop, educational, and sacred. He has written a modern string quartet and music for small ensemble. His music has been performed the world over, including several performances in the historic Assembly Hall on Temple Square in Salt Lake City, Utah. He has maintained a private piano studio for over 40 years. Currently, he lives with his beautiful wife in West Jordan, Utah. He has six children and 17 grandchildren. Kevin has a bachelor's degree in music composition from the University of Utah. He also has Bachelor's and Master's degrees in Special Education. He studied piano performance at the University of Utah with Dr. Bonnie Winterton and composition from Dr. Igor Iachimchuk.

Mark R. Fotheringham has a gift for writing which is regularly neglected in favor of spending time raising his family, the only pursuit producing as much joy as wrangling unruly prose. He writes for a living as Vice President of Communications for the Utah Medical Association, which has honored him with four Distinguished Service Awards. He and his wife of 35 years are the parents of two married daughters and a son who is totally available. They are also grandparents, relentlessly spoiling their progeny with reckless abandon. Many moons ago, Mark graduated magna cum laude from the University of Utah in Journalism & Mass Communications.

Kathryn W. Hales grew up on a farm in southern Idaho, but spent most of her life in Ellensburg, WA on the eastern slopes of the Cascades. She studied at Brigham Young University & graduated from Central Washington University. She & her husband, Ron, now deceased, are the parents of five children, 20 grandchildren & one great-grandchild. Kathryn has taught piano lessons most of her life, starting out as a teenager at 25 cents per lesson. She also enjoys reading, quilting, creative writing, music & growing flowers in her new home in Gig Harbor, Washington.

Mary Ann W. Snowball has spent most of her life in the Salt Lake City area, with a three year hiatus during high school in Eugene, Oregon to pick up her "divinely-appointed" husband of 49 years. She graduated with a Bachelor of Arts degree from Brigham Young University, then went on to mother five living children, and one deceased son who passed away at age five when liver transplants were still in the "experimental" stage. Seventeen grandchildren and two great grandsons have blessed her life since that time. Mary Ann has written poetry from a young age and has had several poems and a true-to-life family history story published by the Church of Jesus Christ of Latter-day Saints. Most of her writing has been dedicated to family members or friends, with words which at times still amaze her--as inspiration is the very best gift when trying to develop a God-given talent. She also enjoys sewing, reading, and learning true doctrine from any source.

20 Ways to Add Variety to the Singing of Hymns

1. Sing the hymns without any variation whatsoever.

2. Combine hymns into a medley of hymns.

3. Change the time signature of a hymn or a verse or section. For example, a hymn in 3-4 time could be changed to 4-4 time by adding an extra beat to each measure.

4. Men, women, or both sing one or more verses in unison.

5. The congregation joins the choir on the final verse or chorus of a hymn. (This is a great way to help the congregation become more familiar with lesser-known hymns.)

6. Women sing one or more verses. Women can sing most hymns in two parts (soprano and alto) or in three parts (soprano, alto, and tenor).

7. Men sing one or more verses. Many hymns can be adapted for use by men's choirs and quartets. One idea is to arrange the voices in the following manner:
    -Baritones (1st basses) sing melody
    -1st Tenors sing alto above the melody
    -2nd Tenors sing Tenor
    -Basses sing Bass
[Men's' choir parts are labeled from highest to lowest voices: 1st Tenor, 2nd Tenor, 1st Bass (Baritone), and 2nd bass. This is often abbreviated TTBB]. Some high notes may need to be adapted. You may also transpose the hymn to a lower key, adapting the bass part.

8. Men sing the hymn with the alto part sung below the melody. When this is done, the bass part is optional.

9. Sopranos and tenors sing a duet for one verse.

10. Tenors and basses sing the melody while the sopranos and altos sing the alto part.

11. One section of the choir sings the melody while the rest of the choir hums or oohs the other parts.

12. The accompanist quietly plays a verse on the piano or organ while someone reads the text to the verse.

13. A soloist sings the melody while the choir hums or oohs the various parts.

14. An instrumental hymn arrangement is played by the piano or organ while the choir or a soloist sings the melody in unison.

15. A piano duet or piano-organ duet is played while the choir or a soloist sings the melody in unison.

16. Men and women alternate singing phrases, in unison or in parts, in a call and response fashion. For example:
Women: Abide with me; 'tis eventide. The day is past and gone;
Men: The shadows of the evening fall; The night is coming on.
Women: Within my heart a welcome guest, Within my home abide.
All together: O Savior, stay this night with me; Behold, 'tis eventide.
Women: O Savior, stay this night with me;
Men: Behold, 'tis eventide.

17. Greatly alter the tempo. For example, sing a hymn very slowly with lots of expression, perhaps pausing briefly at the end of phrases or sections of music.

18. Alter the tempo of one verse or section of a hymn that is normally sung at a fast tempo. Use the text as your guide.

19. Change a section or verse of a hymn to a minor key. Generally, you can flat the 3rd and 6th scale degrees of a song to accomplish this. Sometimes the 7th degree of the scale will sound better flatted as well. For example, a hymn in the key of G Major, uses the notes: G-A-B-C-D-E-F#-G. The G Minor scale is: G-A-Bb-C-D-Eb-F#-G (this is known as Harmonic Minor) or G-A-Bb-C-D-Eb-F-G (this is known as Natural Minor).   This is a wonderful way to highlight a more somber text.

20. Sing the words from one hymn to the music of another. Hymns with similar rhythmic meters sometimes work well with interchanged texts. (See the meter index at the back of some hymnals).

Several of these ideas came from the preface to *Hymns of the Church of Jesus Christ of Latter-day Saints*, 1985.

Pace Music Services